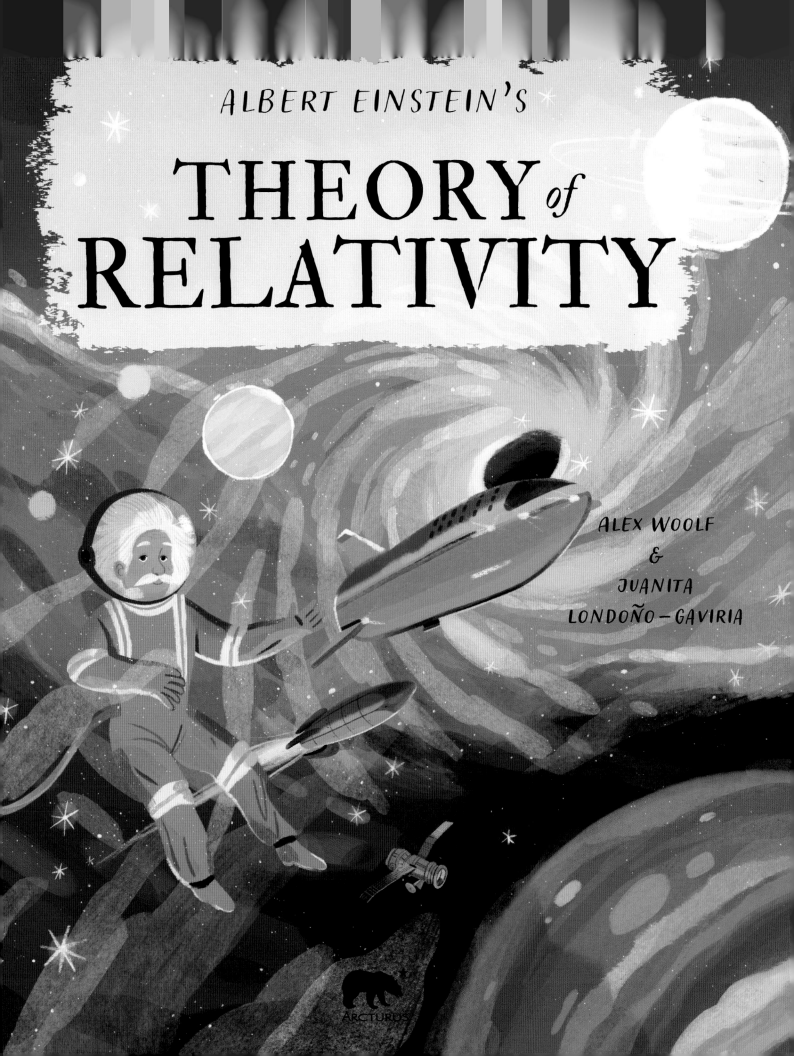

ARCTURUS

This edition published in 2024 by Arcturus Publishing Limited
26/27 Bickels Yard, 151–153 Bermondsey Street,
London SE1 3HA

Writer: Alex Woolf
Illustrator: Juanita Londoño-Gaviria
Designer: Rosie Bellwood
Editors: Becca Clunes, Felicity Forster, and Lydia Halliday
Managing Editor: Joe Harris
Managing Designer: Georgina Wood

ISBN: 978-1-3988-3652-5
CH011054NT
Supplier 29, Date 0124, PI 00004298

Printed in China

ALBERT EINSTEIN'S

THEORY *of* RELATIVITY

INTRODUCTION
SPACE, TIME, AND MOTION

Albert Einstein is one of the most important scientists ever to have lived. In his lifetime, he radically changed the way that people thought about space, time, gravity, and motion.

ALBERT EINSTEIN

Newtonianism

Einstein's wild new ideas flew in the face of some of the most important theories in physics—the laws established by Englishman Isaac Newton (1642–1726). For more than 200 years, Newton's ideas—Newtonian physics—reigned supreme, and were widely regarded as true descriptions of the universe—until Einstein began to question them in the early twentieth century.

ISAAC NEWTON

Absolute Space and Time

To understand the difference between Newton and Einstein, imagine if everything in the universe suddenly disappeared. What would be left? According to Newton, something would still remain—empty space. He believed that space is something that exists with or without objects inside it. Space, to him, was unchanging. Imagine objects in space like points on a page of graph paper— the points on the graph might move, but the grid itself doesn't change. This idea is called "absolute" space.

Newton also believed in absolute time. In an empty universe there would, of course, be no events. You couldn't say this happened before that, because nothing would ever happen. Yet Newton argued that time would still exist, and it would progress at exactly the same steady pace, even if there was nothing to mark its passing. Einstein would come to blow this theory apart, rewriting some of the most important ideas in physics.

The Clockwork Universe

The universe, thankfully for us, is not empty. It is full of objects constantly moving about. Newton developed mathematical laws for how objects move in relation to the forces acting on them—his three laws of motion. One of Newton's greatest discoveries was the universal law of gravitation, which states that there is a force of attraction between all objects related to their masses and the distance between them. Newton's laws of motion and gravitation suggest that objects move in predictable ways. The universe, in this sense, is like a giant piece of clockwork.

Flawed Model

Newton's laws worked—and they still do! We still use them to calculate the orbits of planets, and to send spacecraft to Mars. By the time Einstein was born, Newton's version of physics was still dominant. Yet Newton's model of the universe was flawed. With his own discoveries, Einstein would reveal exactly how Newton got it wrong.

RELATIVITY

A key part of Einstein's idea is relativity—but he didn't come up with that term. The notion had been around since 1632, even before Newton, when Italian scientist Galileo Galilei (1564–1642) published his principle of relativity. It states that the laws of physics are the same whether you are moving or standing still. Therefore, you can never prove that you are in motion. All you can prove is that you are moving faster or slower relative to something else.

GALILEO GALILEI

The Motionless Ship

Imagine that you and a friend are in the cabin of a large ship. The ship is at anchor on a calm sea. In the cabin with you are some butterflies flying around the room. A bottle hanging upside down from the roof drips water into a barrel beneath. You and your friend are tossing a ball to each other.

The Moving Ship

Now imagine the ship sets sail at a steady speed across the smooth sea. You will discover that nothing in the cabin changes. The butterflies still fly at the same speed around the room, the drips from the bottle continue to fall straight down, and you don't need to throw the ball with any more or less force. In other words, there is no physical way of knowing whether the ship is still or moving at a constant speed—the laws of physics remain the same. This led Galileo to conclude that uniform motion and rest are the same thing.

Motion is Relative

To prove this, Galileo would invite you up on deck. There you see another ship alongside yours, moving at exactly the same speed. The ship looks perfectly still, until you look down and observe the foam at its bow as it moves through the water. This demonstrates that motion is relative. If everything in the world moved at the same speed, motion would not exist. Motion only arises when two objects move at different speeds relative to each other.

Galileo's principle of relativity remained a cornerstone of physics until the nineteenth century, when it hit a problem due to new discoveries about electricity, magnetism, and light. Eventually, Einstein worked out how to solve this problem, and came up with a new theory of relativity.

PHYSICS JUST BEFORE EINSTEIN

The physicist who played the biggest part in bringing down Galileo's theory was Scottish mathematician James Clerk Maxwell. He had formulated some equations describing the interactions of electricity and magnetism that seemed to contradict Galileo's principle of relativity.

JAMES CLERK MAXWELL

Maxwell's Discovery

Maxwell's four equations showed that electricity and magnetism were different asepects of the same thing—electromagnetism. Maxwell demonstrated that electromagnetism travels through space as waves, moving at the speed of light (around 300,000 km/s, or 186,000 mi/s). Scientists soon confirmed by experiment that light itself is an electromagnetic wave, along with radio waves, X-rays, and other waves that were discovered later.

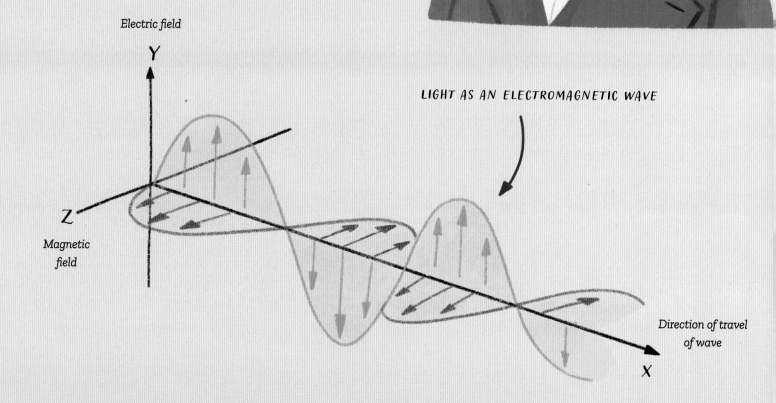

Electric field

Y

Z

Magnetic field

LIGHT AS AN ELECTROMAGNETIC WAVE

Direction of travel of wave

X

The Speed of Light

This caused a major problem with Galileo's ideas. Maxwell's equations stated that light travels at a constant speed in a vacuum. But according to Galileo's principle of relativity, all motion is relative. So if a car is moving at 100 km/h (62 mph), the light from its headlights must travel at the speed of light plus 100 km/h (62 mph). Yet Maxwell said the speed of light never varies. Light speed is not relative.

SPEED OF LIGHT
IS CONSTANT

The Ether

One possible solution to this problem was that light travels through a medium, like sound waves through air. In Galileo's ship (see pages 6–7), sound travels at a constant speed inside the cabin, because the air through which it moves is motionless relative to the ship. (The speed of sound is always the same through still air.) Scientists reasoned that light must therefore also travel through a medium, which they called the ether. The ether was assumed to be a weightless, invisible substance permeating all matter and space. There was just one problem—no one could demonstrate that the ether existed!

The Michelson–Morley Experiment

In 1887, two scientists, Albert Michelson and Edward Morley, carried out an experiment to try to detect the ether. They calculated that if the speed of light was constant relative to the ether, Earth's motion, through the ether could be detected by comparing the speed of light in the direction of Earth's motion with the speed of light at right angles to Earth's motion. No difference was found. The ether had not been detected, and the problem remained.

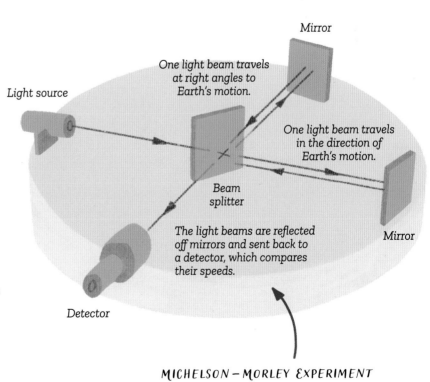

Mirror

Light source

One light beam travels at right angles to Earth's motion.

One light beam travels in the direction of Earth's motion.

Beam splitter

Mirror

The light beams are reflected off mirrors and sent back to a detector, which compares their speeds.

Detector

MICHELSON – MORLEY EXPERIMENT

ABOUT EINSTEIN
EARLY LIFE

Albert Einstein was born on March 14th, 1879, in Ulm, Germany, to a Jewish family. Six weeks later, his parents moved to the city of Munich. Albert was very slow at learning how to speak. His parents were worried enough to consult a doctor about it, and the family maid began calling him "der Depperte" (the dopey one).

Top in Mathematics

At age five, Albert's father gave him a magnetic compass. He was fascinated by the invisible forces that could move the needle, and would remain inrigued for the rest of his life. In his early school years, Albert was top of his class at mathematics. By the age of twelve, his parents had bought him geometry and science books, so that he could study the subjects he enjoyed most outside of school as well.

Riding Alongside a Light Beam

Albert preferred to think in pictures rather than in words. At the age of sixteen, he tried to picture what it would be like to travel fast enough to catch up with a light beam. If he rode alongside it, the light wave would appear motionless. Yet he knew this was impossible, because Maxwell's equations showed that the speed of light was constant (always stayed the same) and so could never appear motionless (see pages 8–9). This contradiction made him very uncomfortable. For the next ten years he wrestled with the problem, until he came up with his special theory of relativity.

Finding His Way

Following a brief stint living in Italy, Albert moved to Zurich, Switzerland, in 1896, where he went to a technical college to study mathematics and physics. Albert didn't study very hard at college and his professors refused to recommend him to employers. He tried and failed to get work as a laboratory assistant. In 1902, he got a job at a government patent office in the Swiss capital, Bern. It was here that he came up with the ideas that would change physics forever.

AT COLLEGE, ALBERT MET AND FELL IN LOVE WITH A FELLOW STUDENT, MILEVA MARIĆ, WHO HE WOULD MARRY IN 1903 AND LATER HAVE TWO CHILDREN WITH.

1905: EINSTEIN'S MIRACLE YEAR

Einstein's task at the patent office was to assess applications for patents—licenses giving someone the exclusive right to make and sell their invention. He found the job easy, and it left him with plenty of spare time to think. Some of the inventions he assessed may even have inspired his thinking.

Annals of Physics

Einstein began to write scientific essays (or papers) and send them to a journal, *Annalen der Physik* (*Annals of Physics*). During his first three years at the patent office, Einstein published around one essay each year. In 1905, the year he turned 26, he published four essays. This was later called his "year of miracles," because each of these essays turned out to be a major contribution to physics—and two of them completely revolutionized our understanding of space, time, mass, and energy.

The Photoelectric Effect

The first of Einstein's famous essays of 1905 explained the photoelectric effect. It proposed the idea that light could exist as separate packets, or particles, of energy (later called photons). It was for this work that Einstein would later win a Nobel Prize.

Brownian Motion

The second essay looked at Brownian motion, the random way that microscopic particles move in a fluid. This paper helped to prove the existence of atoms and molecules by enabling scientists to indirectly observe their activity during experiments.

Theory of Relativity

In his third essay, Einstein introduced his special theory of relativity (see pages 20–21), which dealt with light and its relationship with time and space, solving the problem that had been haunting physics ever since Maxwell came up with his equations (see pages 8–9).

Famous Equation

The fourth essay explored a consequence of the special theory of relativity, which is that mass and energy are different forms of the same thing. He expressed this in what would become the most famous equation in all of science: $E = mc^2$.

ACADEMIC SUCCESS

It did not take long for Einstein's name to become known by the world's top physicists. The papers he published in 1905 were so bold and grand in scope that, even if they were not yet fully accepted, they could not help but capture attention.

Climbing the Ladder

Soon, physicists began visiting Einstein in Bern, hoping to work with him. It helped Einstein's status that in 1906 he received his PhD, a degree awarded to students who complete a long essay that offers a significant contribution to their subject. Now, he would be called Dr Einstein. In 1908, he left his job at the patent office and began climbing the academic ladder, accepting positions at a range of prestigious universities in Bern, Switzerland; Zurich, Switzerland; Prague, Czech Republic; and Berlin, Germany. By 1911, he had become Professor Einstein.

Scientific Breakthroughs

Meanwhile, Einstein continued his research into relativity. In 1907, he developed the equivalence principle (see pages 28–29), and in 1915, he completed what is often considered his masterpiece, the general theory of relativity (see pages 30–31).

War

In 1914, World War I broke out. Many prominent German intellectuals signed a document called "Manifesto of the Ninety-Three," proclaiming their support for the war. Einstein was one of the few who refused to sign. Instead, he put his name to another document, "Manifesto to the Europeans," which pushed for peace. He would write, "At such a time as this, one realizes what a sorry species of animal one belongs to." Throughout his life, Einstein would remain a pacifist (someone who believes that all war is unjustifiable).

Divorce and Remarriage

As his fame spread, Einstein's marriage to Mileva Marić began to fall apart. He was often away at conferences or lost in thoughts about relativity, and the couple often argued. In 1912, Einstein began a relationship with his cousin Elsa Löwenthal. In 1919, he and Mileva got divorced, and three months later, Einstein married Elsa.

EINSTEIN WITH HIS SECOND WIFE ELSA LÖWENTHAL.

WORLDWIDE FAME

Einstein's general theory of relativity predicted that starlight would be bent near the Sun due to the effect of gravity on light. This could only be seen during a solar eclipse. In 1919, photographs were taken of a solar eclipse in order to test Einstein's theory, which was proved to be correct! The significance of this discovery was widely reported in the media. Almost overnight, Einstein became the most famous scientist in the world.

Einstein and Charlie Chaplin

Nobel Prize

The Times newspaper in London hailed the theory of relativity as a "Revolution in Science" and declared that "Newton's ideas [had been] overthrown." Einstein received letters from institutions all around the world inviting him to speak about his theories. In 1922, he was awarded the Nobel Prize for Physics, but not for his relativity theories. The Nobel committee suspected that these might be wrong. Instead, they gave it to him for his work on the photoelectric effect (see pages 46–47).

World Tours

Between 1921 and 1923, Einstein undertook several international speaking tours, visiting the USA, Britain, France, Spain, Singapore, Ceylon (now Sri Lanka), Japan, and Palestine (now Israel). Everywhere he went, he was greeted by crowds numbering in the thousands. In Japan, he met with the emperor and empress at the Imperial Palace. In Spain, he received a diploma from the king. In 1925, he toured South America, visiting Argentina, Uruguay, and Brazil.

Back in America

In 1930–31, Einstein made a return trip to the USA. In New York, the audience cheered him during a visit to the opera house, and the president of Columbia University described him as "the ruling monarch of the mind." In California, Einstein met the movie star Charlie Chaplin, and they immediately got along. At the premiere of Chaplin's latest film, they were mobbed by the crowd. Chaplin remarked, "The people applaud me because everybody understands me, and they applaud you because no one understands you."

LATER LIFE

The 1930s were difficult for Einstein. His son Eduard suffered a mental breakdown in 1930 and would spend the rest of his life in an institution. Einstein's beloved wife Elsa died in 1936. He also witnessed the rise of the anti-Jewish Nazi Party in Germany, the land of his birth. In October 1933, Einstein took up a position at the Institute for Advanced Study at Princeton, USA, where he would remain for the rest of his life. In 1940, he became an American citizen.

I made one great mistake in my life—when I signed the letter to President Roosevelt recommending that atom bombs be made; but there was some justification—the danger that the Germans would make them.

Albert Einstein, recorded by Linus Pauling in "Note to self regarding a meeting with Albert Einstein, November 16, 1954".

Book Burnings

In 1933, the Nazis began introducing anti-Jewish laws. They organized book burnings of works by Jewish authors, including Einstein. They condemned relativity as "Jewish physics" and enlisted one hundred scientists to denounce it. Einstein said that defeating relativity did not need one hundred scientists, just one fact.

The Bomb

Einstein had previously noted that his equation $E = mc^2$ might lead to the creation of an extremely powerful bomb (see pages 40–41). As a lifelong pacifist, he was appalled that physicists in the 1930s were seriously contemplating how to build such a weapon, known as an atomic bomb. Einstein's biggest fear was that the Nazis would build one first. In July 1939, Hungarian-American physicist Leo Szilard convinced Einstein to send a letter to US President Franklin Roosevelt, urging him to develop a bomb to counter the Nazi threat. The letter paved the way for the Manhattan Project—the project to build the world's first atomic bomb.

Einstein deeply regretted writing a letter to President Roosevelt encouraging him to make an atom bomb.

Final Years

In his later years, Einstein continued his scientific research, but became increasingly isolated from the physics community. Most physicists by this time were working on quantum theory (see pages 44–45), which Einstein had helped establish with his work on the photoelectric effect. Einstein struggled to accept quantum theory, partly because the laws governing the quantum world conflicted with those of general relativity. He was determined to discover a "theory of everything" that would unify all the forces in the universe (see pages 60–61). Sadly, he was unable to achieve this goal. On April 17, 1955, Albert Einstein died due to internal bleeding from an artery in his abdomen.

EINSTEIN'S THEORIES
THE SPECIAL THEORY OF RELATIVITY

The Michelson–Morley experiment of 1887 (see page 9) threw the world of physics into confusion, having shown there was no ether. The speed of light was constant, contradicting Galileo's principle of relativity. The world's top physicists put their minds to the problem—resulting in some rather unusual theories. A pair of scientists willing to think outside the box—Hendrik Lorentz of the Netherlands and Henri Poincaré of France—very nearly solved the problem.

Lorentz suggested that objects start to shrink along their length when approaching light speed.

Lorentz and Poincaré

Lorentz suggested that objects must shrink when they move, and the shrinking is along the direction of motion, so a car moving forward would lose length but not height. The faster the car travels, the more it shrinks, and the shrinking is exactly as much as is needed to keep the speed of light measurement constant. Poincaré realized that time, too, must move slower for objects in motion. He asked Lorentz to adjust his equations.

Strange Idea

These ideas seemed utterly bizarre to physicists. Lorentz's equations worked mathematically, but few believed they had any connection with reality. Poincaré gave a lecture on the subject in 1904, ending with the hope that physicists might create a new principle of relativity that encompassed light. Little did he know that just a year later an unknown patent clerk in Bern would do exactly that.

The Clock Tower

Every morning during the spring of 1905, Einstein would walk to work with his friend and colleague Michele Besso, and they would discuss the problem obsessing the world of physics. One evening in May 1905, Einstein found himself gazing up at the clock tower in the middle of Bern and imagining an impossible scene. What would happen, he wondered, if he raced away from the clock tower at the speed of light? The light from the clock would not be able to catch up with him. The clock, and time itself, would appear to have stopped. How could that be? That was when the solution suddenly struck him—time is relative—it can stretch and shrink. Lorentz and Poincaré had made time flexible simply to make the mathematics work—Einstein saw that time really did change. Six weeks later, he completed his essay on the special theory of relativity.

TIME IS RELATIVE

In his essay on special relativity, Einstein explained that time is relative, which means that people moving at different speeds experience time differently. The faster you travel, the slower you move through time relative to a stationary person. How is that possible? To understand this, let's try a thought experiment...

The Speeding Train

Imagine riding on a train at 100 km/h (62 mph). A train on a parallel track overtakes you at 130 km/h (80 mph). From your point of view, it appears to be moving at 30 km/h (18 mph). Now imagine your train accelerates to 100,000 km/s (62,000 mi/s), one-third of the speed of light. A light beam shone alongside your train would, logic suggests, pass you at 200,000 km/s (124,000 mi/s), the speed of light minus your own speed. Yet when you measure the speed of that light beam with a stopwatch, it's moving at 300,000 km/s (186,000 mi/s)—the speed of light. It doesn't matter how fast you travel, it will always measure the same because light speed is constant.

The Slowing Stopwatch

There is a contradiction here: you're moving at one-third the speed of light, yet your stopwatch still shows the light beam moving at the speed of light. Einstein understood that there can only be one solution to this paradox: your stopwatch—and your motion through time—has slowed down. It doesn't appear to have slowed down from your point of view, but to anyone stationary observing your stopwatch, they would see it running slow.

Why Don't We Notice It?

Einstein had discovered that the faster we travel through space, the slower time moves for us. This is known as "time dilation". So why don't we notice it? How is it that we can all agree what the time is, whether we're moving or still? How is it that we're able to catch trains and arrive at meetings on time? It's because the slowing of time is extremely small at the speeds we travel at. It only becomes noticeable when we approach the speed of light.

SPACE IS RELATIVE

In his explanation of the Michelson–Morley experiment, Hendrik Lorentz had suggested the strange idea of length contraction—that objects shrink as they move. He did this to make his equations work.

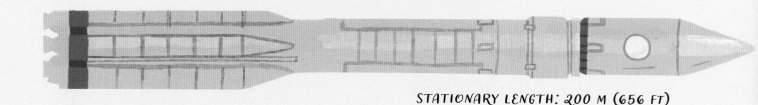

STATIONARY LENGTH: 200 M (656 FT)

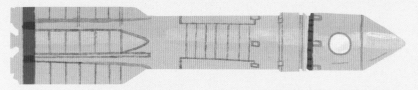

AT 86.5 PERCENT OF LIGHT SPEED:
100 M (328 FT)

Length Contraction

A spaceship moving close to light speed would appear shorter to a stationary observer because the light from the front and rear of the spaceship will reach the observer's eyes at slightly different times. For an astronaut aboard the spaceship, it would still be the same length as when stationary.

AT 99 PERCENT OF LIGHT SPEED:
28 M (92 FT)

AT 99.99 PERCENT OF LIGHT SPEED:
3 M (10 FT)

Newton was Wrong!

Einstein's special theory of relativity explained the Michelson–Morley experiment. He showed that there was no need for the ether (see page 9), and that Galileo's principle of relativity could also include light. In doing so, Einstein demonstrated that Newton's idea of absolute space and time was wrong (see pages 4–5). Space and time change, depending on motion. It is the speed of light that is absolute.

Space-motion and Time-motion

Einstein was the first person to understand the special relationship between space and time. When you're standing still, you're not moving through space but you continue to move through time. We could say that all of your motion is through time. As you start to move, some of your motion through time changes to motion through space. The faster you move, the more of your time-motion gets converted to space-motion, which is why your time-motion appears slower to a motionless observer. At light speed, all time-motion is converted to space-motion, and to anyone watching, your time would appear to stand still.

TIME

STATIONARY OBJECT

MOVING OBJECT

SPEED OF LIGHT

SPACE

Spacetime

Einstein had shown that time and space aren't separate, but one thing. German mathematician Hermann Minkowski, a former teacher of Einstein, coined the term "spacetime" to describe this idea. Spacetime has four dimensions—three dimensions of space, and one of time. The concept may sound strange, but we use spacetime in our everyday lives. If you ask a friend to meet you in a café on the fourth floor of a building on Third Street at 5 pm, you are telling them where to meet you in spacetime.

HERMANN MINKOWSKI

Hermann Minkowski made a huge contribution towards Einstein's theory of relativity.

THE FAMOUS EQUATION

Soon after publishing his essay, Einstein realized something else about relativity—something that would have huge ramifications for physics and the world. He quickly wrote another essay to set out his idea. This essay, just three pages long, was published in November 1905. It explained that mass, like time and space, is relative, and that mass and energy are different forms of the same thing. Einstein summarized this idea in a simple yet powerful equation: $E = mc^2$.

What Does it Mean?

In Einstein's equation, "E" means energy, "m" means mass, and "c" means the speed of light. So he is saying that energy equals mass times the speed of light squared. The speed of light squared is an enormous number (90,000,000,000 km/s, or 56,000,000,000 mi/s), which means that just a tiny amount of mass is equivalent to a vast amount of energy.

What is Mass?

How did Einstein arrive at this conclusion? It helps first of all to understand what he meant by mass. In everyday language, mass is another word for weight, but to a physicist mass is a measurement of inertia—an object's resistance to being moved. The bigger an object's mass, the harder it is to move.

Changes with Acceleration

Einstein noticed that an object uses energy to accelerate (go faster). At the same time, its mass (or resistance to further acceleration) increases as it goes faster. So energy is being converted into mass. At normal speeds, these gains are tiny. A bird in flight has very slightly more mass than when it was perched on a branch, but the increase is billions of times smaller than the mass of one of its feathers.

Approaching Light Speed

As an object approaches the speed of light, its mass increases dramatically. If an object ever reached light speed, its mass would become infinite (limitless in size). The bigger an object's mass, the more energy it takes to move it. Therefore, an infinite mass would need an infinite amount of energy to accelerate. This is obviously impossible, which is why nothing can go faster than light.

Bomb Proof

Just as a huge amount of energy converts to a tiny amount of mass, so a tiny amount of mass can potentially be converted into a huge amount of energy. Forty years after Einstein's findings, the USA dropped atomic bombs on the Japanese cities of Hiroshima and Nagasaki during World War II—a devastating proof that Einstein was right about this.

EINSTEIN'S HAPPIEST THOUGHT

Einstein was unsatisfied with his theory of special relativity, because it only dealt with objects in uniform motion—objects moving in a straight line at a steady speed. He wanted to extend relativity to include accelerated motion. This set him on a path towards his general theory of relativity, which he would eventually complete in 1915.

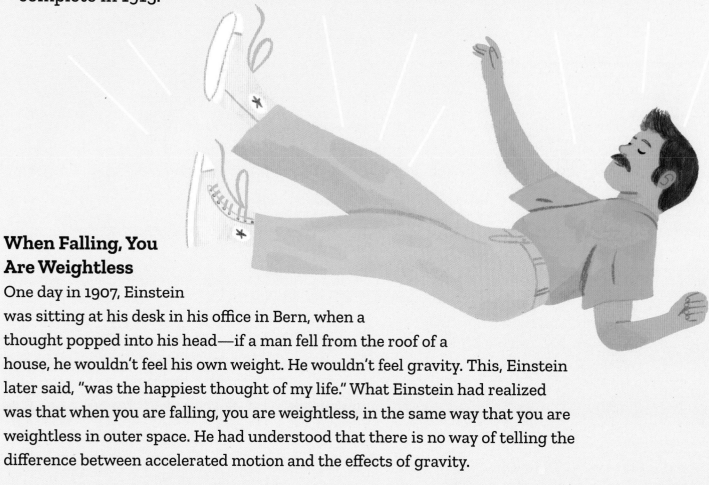

When Falling, You Are Weightless

One day in 1907, Einstein was sitting at his desk in his office in Bern, when a thought popped into his head—if a man fell from the roof of a house, he wouldn't feel his own weight. He wouldn't feel gravity. This, Einstein later said, "was the happiest thought of my life." What Einstein had realized was that when you are falling, you are weightless, in the same way that you are weightless in outer space. He had understood that there is no way of telling the difference between accelerated motion and the effects of gravity.

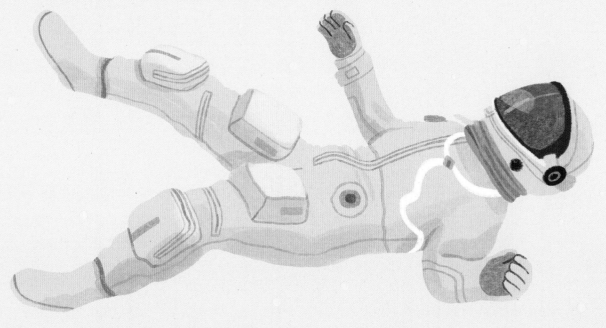

Dropping a Ball in Space

To understand why this is important, imagine a spaceship accelerating through space. It is accelerating at the precise rate to give the astronauts the sensation of gravity on Earth, 9.8 m/s² (32.2 ft/s²). If an astronaut lets go of a ball, it will fall to the spaceship's floor at exactly the same speed as it would do on Earth. This is because the floor of the spacecraft is accelerating towards the object. Now imagine the spaceship is a self-flying craft with no portholes and silent engines. The astronauts would have no idea whether they were moving in space or stationary on Earth.

Gravity and Accelerated Motion

Einstein called his idea "the equivalence principle," because it revealed the equivalence between gravity and accelerated motion. On the spaceship, the gravity effect only exists while the acceleration exists. When the spaceship slows down, the sensation of gravity disappears. According to Einstein, the gravity felt aboard the spaceship is indistinguishable from the gravity felt on Earth.

A GENERAL THEORY OF RELATIVITY

Einstein knew that his equivalence principle was the key to developing a general theory of relativity. He could construct a theory involving acceleration and know that it would also apply to gravity. With this in mind, he came up with a new thought experiment ...

The Spinning Disk

Acceleration isn't just forward motion—it's an increase in speed in any direction. Imagine you and a friend are standing on a spinning disk with a wall at its edge. You tie yourself to a post in the middle of the disk, but your friend does not. As the disk rotates faster (accelerates), your friend gets pulled out toward the edge and is pinned against the wall. You, being secured to your post in the middle, feel hardly any movement compared to her. If the disk is big enough and rotating fast enough, you will notice certain changes. You will see your friend getting thinner —her length reducing in the direction of motion. This is known as length contraction. You will also see her clock ticking more slowly. This is known as time dilation.

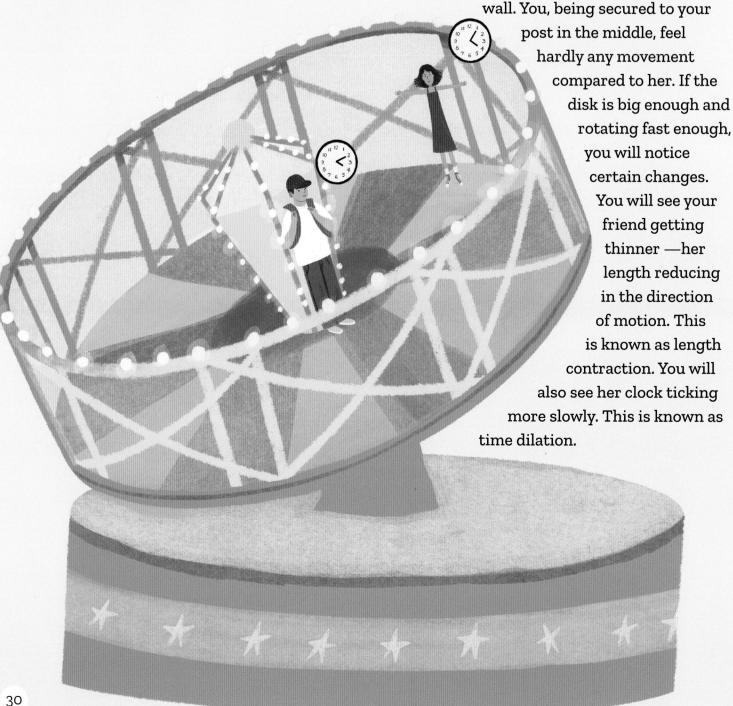

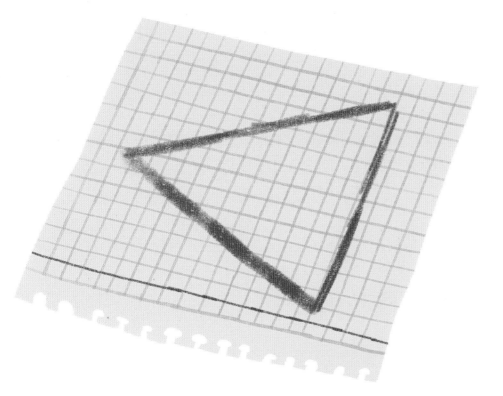

Gravity Warps Spacetime

The spinning disk thought experiment showed Einstein that accelerated motion warps (curves) both space and time—or spacetime. According to the equivalence principle, the effects of acceleration and gravity are indistinguishable. Therefore, he concluded that gravity warps spacetime.

To describe the warping of spacetime mathematically, Einstein needed a type of geometry that worked on curved surfaces.

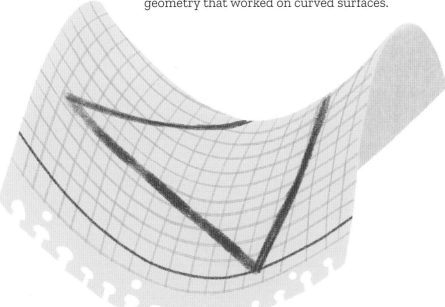

Geometry of Curves

To work this out mathematically was going to be complicated. The geometry we learn at school uses flat surfaces. If Einstein was going to find a theory of relativity that included gravity, he would need a different sort of geometry: one that works on curved surfaces. His friend, Swiss mathematician Marcel Grossmann, introduced him to Riemannian geometry, which does exactly that.

A New Theory of Gravity

Using this form of geometry, Einstein was able to develop equations that described a new theory of gravity, entirely different to Newton's. He had managed, after ten years of struggle, to complete his general theory of relativity, often described as one of the most beautiful theories in all of science.

WARPED SPACETIME

In his general theory of relativity, Einstein suggested a new way of understanding gravity—not as a force, but as a warping (curving) of spacetime, caused by massive bodies affecting the motion of other bodies around them. As usual, the best way to understand what Einstein meant is by thinking of it visually.

The Rubber Sheet

Imagine spacetime as a large, flexible rubber sheet stretched tight on all sides so that it is completely flat. If you place something heavy, like a bowling ball, onto the sheet, it will create a big dip in the surface. If you then place a tennis ball onto the sheet, it will roll toward the bowling ball. The bowling ball isn't pulling the tennis ball toward it. The tennis ball moves toward it because of the curvature of the sheet created by the bowling ball. The greater the mass of the bowling ball, the more it warps the sheet, and the more any other smaller balls will move toward it.

I think in four dimensions, but only abstractly. The human mind can picture these dimensions no more than it can envisage electricity.

Albert Einstein, from an interview in *The Saturday Evening Post* (October 26, 1929).

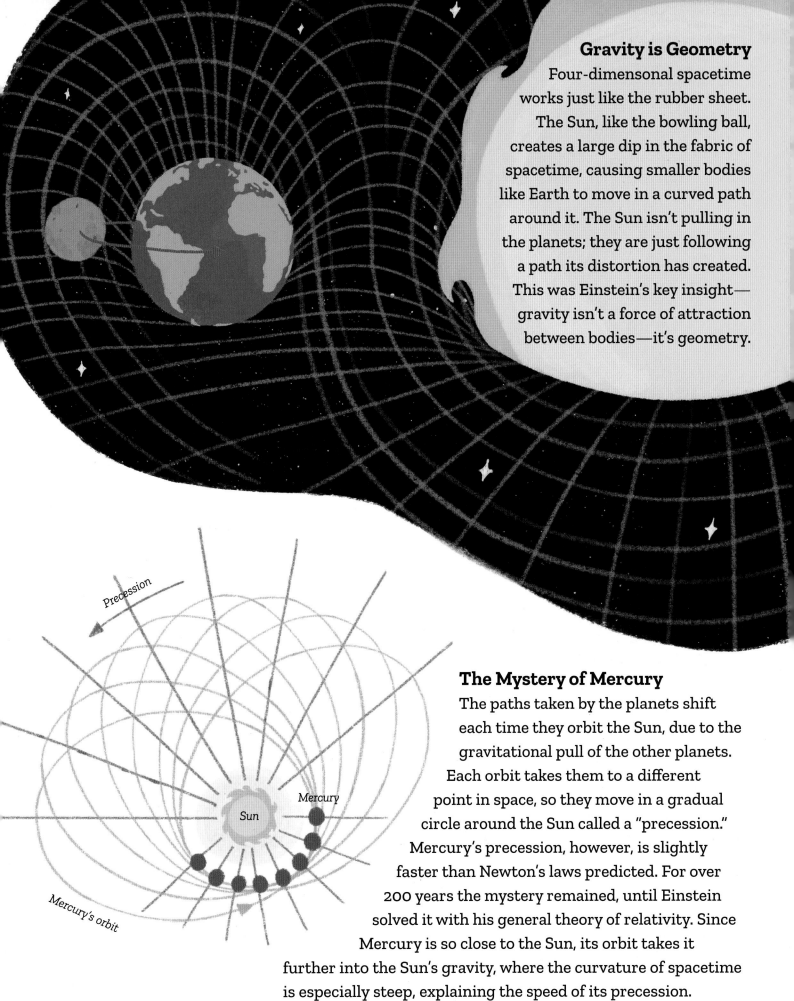

Gravity is Geometry

Four-dimensional spacetime works just like the rubber sheet. The Sun, like the bowling ball, creates a large dip in the fabric of spacetime, causing smaller bodies like Earth to move in a curved path around it. The Sun isn't pulling in the planets; they are just following a path its distortion has created. This was Einstein's key insight— gravity isn't a force of attraction between bodies—it's geometry.

The Mystery of Mercury

The paths taken by the planets shift each time they orbit the Sun, due to the gravitational pull of the other planets. Each orbit takes them to a different point in space, so they move in a gradual circle around the Sun called a "precession." Mercury's precession, however, is slightly faster than Newton's laws predicted. For over 200 years the mystery remained, until Einstein solved it with his general theory of relativity. Since Mercury is so close to the Sun, its orbit takes it further into the Sun's gravity, where the curvature of spacetime is especially steep, explaining the speed of its precession.

33

GRAVITY BENDS LIGHT

Some interesting consequences arose from Einstein's general theory of relativity, demonstrating that the universe is a lot stranger than it appears. Take light, for example. It has no mass, so surely it cannot be affected by gravity? Not true. Light may have no mass, but a massive body can bend a beam of light by warping the spacetime through which it travels.

The Light Beam in the Spaceship

Einstein actually realized this back in 1907, when he discovered the equivalence of accelerated motion and gravity (see pages 28–29). To understand how, imagine a spaceship accelerating through space. The spaceship has a very small window admitting a thin beam of light. Because the spaceship is accelerating while the light is passing through it, the light will strike the opposite wall slightly lower down. So the path of the beam has to bend very slightly during its journey from window to wall. Since gravity and accelerated motion are equivalent, gravity must also bend light.

A light beam bends very slightly as it passes through the window of an accelerating spaceship.

Proving the Theory

Einstein realized that one way of proving whether his general theory of relativity was correct would be to see if a massive body, like the Sun, could indeed bend a beam of light. Could the Sun bend the light coming from a star in a nearby part of the sky? During daylight hours, the Sun is too bright for us to see the stars. But there is a time when this effect can be observed, and that is during a solar eclipse, when the Moon obscures the Sun.

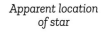

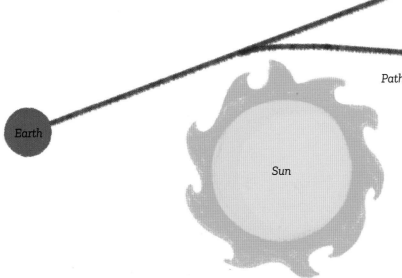

Apparent location of star

Path of starlight

Actual location of star

Earth

Sun

The Sun can cause the light coming from a nearby star to bend.

ARTHUR EDDINGTON

Expedition

In 1919, astronomer Arthur Eddington decided to test Einstein's theory by going to the island of Principe, off the west coast of Africa, to observe a solar eclipse. The day of the eclipse, May 29, was cloudy. When the eclipse began at 3.13 pm, the stars couldn't be seen. Then, for a few brief moments, the stars appeared. Eddington took 16 photographs, five of which showed stars. Back in England, he developed the photographs and took careful measurements. The results showed that light from the stars had been deflected (bent) by the exact amount that Einstein had predicted in his equations.

GRAVITY SLOWS TIME

We have seen how the warping of spacetime, which we call gravity, can affect the movement of physical things like planets, as well as light. With his theory, Einstein showed how gravity can also affect the movement of time. The stronger the gravitational pull, the more slowly time moves.

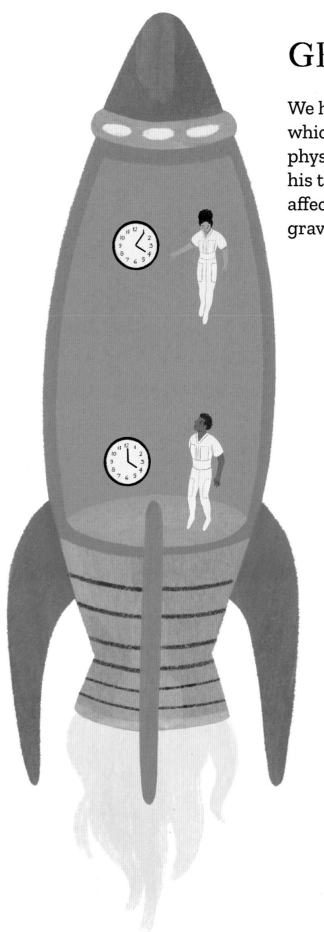

Clocks on a Spaceship

To understand how this is possible, let's look first at the effect of acceleration on time. Imagine an extremely long spaceship accelerating through space. Jane is at the front of the ship and Fred is at the back. They both have clocks that are set at the same time. While the light from Fred's clock travels to Jane's eyes, the spaceship will have moved slightly further on, so to Jane, Fred's clock appears to run slow. Fred will experience the opposite: as the light from Jane's clock travels toward his eyes, the spaceship will have moved him closer to it, so her clock will appear to run fast.

An accelerating spaceship will affect the rate at which time moves. The faster it accelerates, the slower time will pass.

Doppler Effect

Because Jane is moving away from Fred's clock, the light waves reaching her eyes get stretched out, with fewer waves per second, causing the clock to appear to run slow. Fred is rushing toward Jane's clock, causing the light waves reaching his eyes to become compressed, making her clock appear to run fast. This is known as the "Doppler effect". You experience it yourself with sound waves when you hear an ambulance go by. The pitch of the siren rises as it approaches you and the sound waves become compressed, and lowers as the vehicle moves away and the sound waves become stretched out.

LONG WAVELENGTH CAUSES A LOW-PITCHED SOUND

SHORT WAVELENGTH CAUSES A HIGH-PITCHED SOUND

Clocks on Earth

We know from the equivalence principle (see pages 28–29) that acceleration and gravity are equivalent, so gravity must distort time in the same way as our accelerating spaceship. In fact, the whole experiment could have taken place on Earth. Time will move more slowly the closer you are to the ground, where Earth's gravitational pull is stronger. Scientists proved this in 1960. Clocks were placed at the top and bottom of a 24 m (79 ft) building at Harvard University in the USA. The difference in the speed of time was extremely small, but measurable.

WEAKER GRAVITY

STRONGER GRAVITY

Time will move ever so slightly faster at the top of a mountain, where Earth's gravity is weaker, than it will at the bottom.

EINSTEIN'S LEGACY
WAS EINSTEIN RIGHT?

Einstein's theories of relativity work beautifully in terms of mathematics, but do they reflect reality? Testing them is not easy, as the effects are most noticeable at extreme speeds, beyond anything humans are capable of. Nevertheless, they have been tested many times using very precise measuring tools, and their predictions have proved accurate in all cases.

At times I feel certain I am right while not knowing the reason ... Imagination is more important than knowledge. For knowledge is limited, whereas imagination embraces the entire world.

Albert Einstein, *Cosmic Religion: With Other Opinions and Aphorisms* (1931).

Muons

Special relativity has been proved by the example of the muon. Muons are tiny particles that form in our atmosphere 6,000 m (20,000 ft) up. They exist for an average of 2.2 microseconds and travel toward Earth at 99.8 percent of the speed of light. Moving at this speed, they should drop just 660 m (2,100 ft), never reaching Earth's surface. Yet we detect them reaching ground level all the time. That's because of time dilation. Relative to us, muons exist for 34.8 microseconds, more than enough time for them to reach the surface.

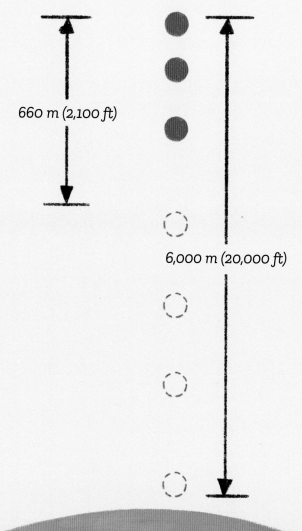

660 m (2,100 ft)

6,000 m (20,000 ft)

Muons exist for such a short time, they should not be able to reach Earth's surface. The fact that we can detect them there proves that time dilation, predicted by Einstein's special theory of relativity, is real.

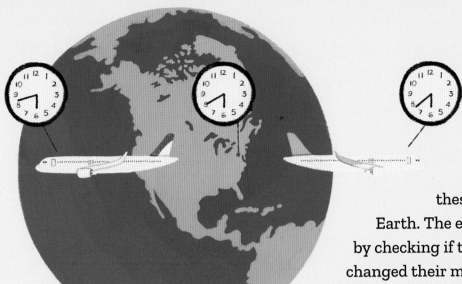

Clocks on Planes

In 1971, scientists set up an experiment to test both the special and general theories of relativity. They put extremely accurate clocks aboard two planes and compared these to an equally accurate clock on Earth. The experiment tested special relativity by checking if the planes' motion through space changed their motion through time relative to the clock on Earth. It tested general relativity by checking if Earth's gravity slowed the surface clock relative to the clocks on the planes. The result was that one plane lost a tiny amount of time and one gained a tiny amount of time compared to the ground clock. These results agreed very well with Einstein's theories.

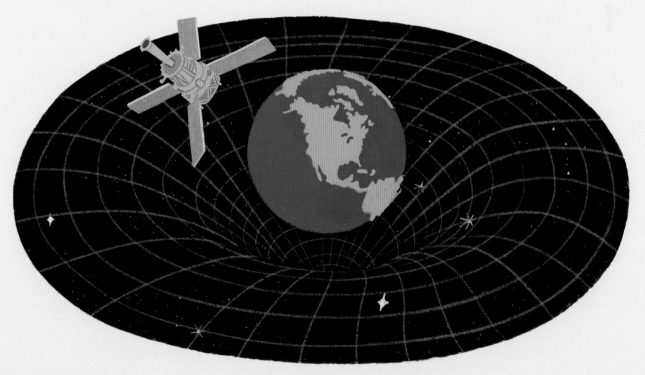

Gravity Probe B

Starting in April 2004, the satellite Gravity Probe B (GP-B) circled Earth from pole to pole for 17 months, taking careful measurements. Its job was to test two aspects of general relativity—firstly, whether Earth's gravity warps spacetime, and secondly, an effect known as "frame-dragging." To understand frame-dragging, imagine the Earth floating in honey. As it spins, the honey around it would swirl—well, so should spacetime, according to general relativity. The ultra-sensitive equipment aboard GP-B confirmed both the warping of spacetime and frame-dragging, just as Einstein's theories predicted.

NUCLEAR POWER

In his final essay of 1905, Einstein showed that mass and energy are equivalent, as described by his famous equation $E = mc^2$ (see pages 26–27). This led some scientists to wonder if there might be a way to get at the energy locked up inside an atom's nucleus (central core). Scientists achieved this in the 1940s with the atomic bomb, using a process called "nuclear fission."

A nuclear fission reaction

Neutron

Target nucleus

Neutron

Lighter element

Lighter element

Neutron

Neutron

OTTO FRISCH AND LISE MEITNER, WHO DISCOVERED NUCLEAR FISSION.

Nuclear Fission

The nucleus of almost every atom is made up of particles called protons and neutrons. Scientists discovered that by firing a neutron at an atom of uranium-235 (a form of the element uranium), it splits the nucleus, releasing neutrons and lighter elements. This process, called nuclear fission, converts some of the atom's mass into energy, as predicted by $E = mc^2$. The neutrons that were released struck other uranium-235 atoms and split them, releasing more neutrons, and so on. This is called a chain reaction. The amount of energy generated can be enormous. The first atomic bomb had the power of around 40,000 conventional bombs, and was produced by a chunk of uranium-235 that could fit inside a coffee mug.

Power Stations

With atomic bombs, the fission chain reaction is extremely rapid and uncontrolled. Scientists soon discovered ways of controlling the reaction to create a safe form of energy. Rods of the element (usually uranium-238) are pushed toward each other until a controlled amount of heat is produced. This heats water, producing steam that drives a turbine to produce electricity.

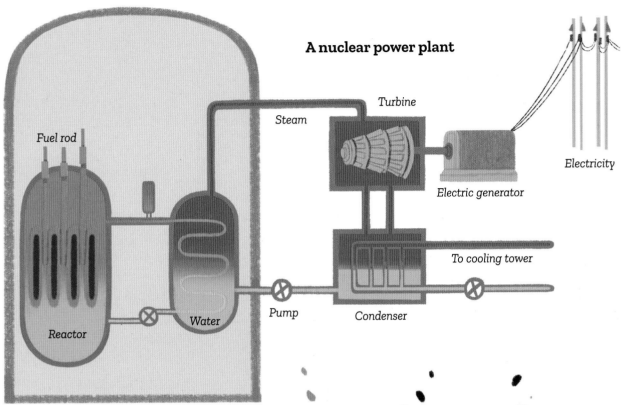

A nuclear power plant

Fuel rod

Turbine

Steam

Electricity

Electric generator

To cooling tower

Reactor

Water

Pump

Condenser

Nuclear Fusion

Until Einstein came up with his equation $E = mc^2$, the source of the Sun's energy was a mystery. We now know that the Sun converts its mass into energy through a process called "nuclear fusion." Unlike fission, which involves splitting the nuclei of atoms, this involves fusing atoms to release energy. Fusing atoms is hard because they contain protons, positively charged

particles that repel each other. Nuclear fusion requires enormous amounts of heat and pressure, conditions that occur inside the Sun. Scientists and engineers are trying to build nuclear fusion reactors. Once the technology has been perfected, these could provide a clean, cheap form of energy.

EINSTEIN AND THE UNIVERSE

After Einstein completed his general theory of relativity, he began using it as a tool to discover the nature of the universe. In February 1917, he published a paper presenting a new model of the universe. It differed in many ways from the universe described by Isaac Newton (see pages 4–5).

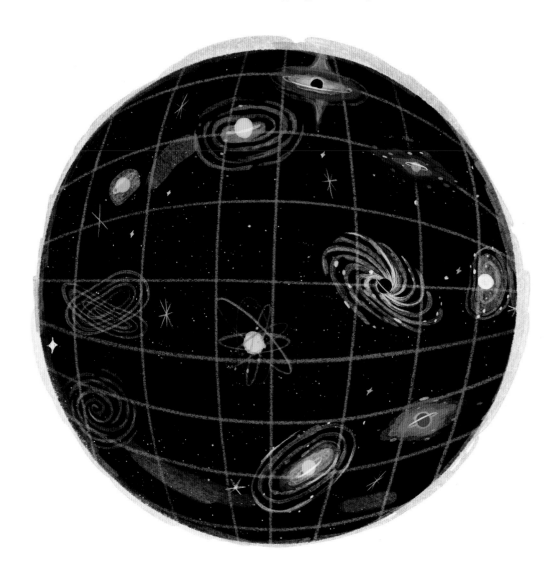

Finite and Unbounded

Newton had believed in an infinite, eternal, unchanging universe. In Einstein's view, the universe is finite, yet unbounded (it has no edge). To explain this apparent contradiction, he asked us to imagine the three dimensions of space as a flat, two-dimensional surface formed into a sphere. Any two-dimensional being moving across this surface will never find an edge. If it travels far enough in one direction, it will eventually end up where it started. Einstein's model of the universe is a three-dimensional version of this sphere—unbounded, yet finite.

The Cosmological Constant

Einstein did, however, share Newton's belief that the universe is a stable size and eternal, with no beginning or end. He was therefore disturbed when his equations predicted an expanding or collapsing universe. This did not accord with what astronomers thought at the time, so Einstein decided to adjust his model to agree with reality. He added a term to his equations called the "cosmological constant." This was a force of repulsion to counterbalance gravity, keeping the universe static.

His "Biggest Blunder"

Unfortunately for Einstein, in 1929, just 12 years after he published his model, American astronomer Edwin Hubble confirmed the theories that the universe is not a stable size. In fact, it's expanding. This suggested that the universe isn't eternal, but had a beginning, later known as the "Big Bang." Einstein realized he had been wrong to add the cosmological constant. He should have trusted his equations. He called this his "biggest blunder." However, in a strange twist, it turns out Einstein may have been right after all. See pages 56–57 to find out why.

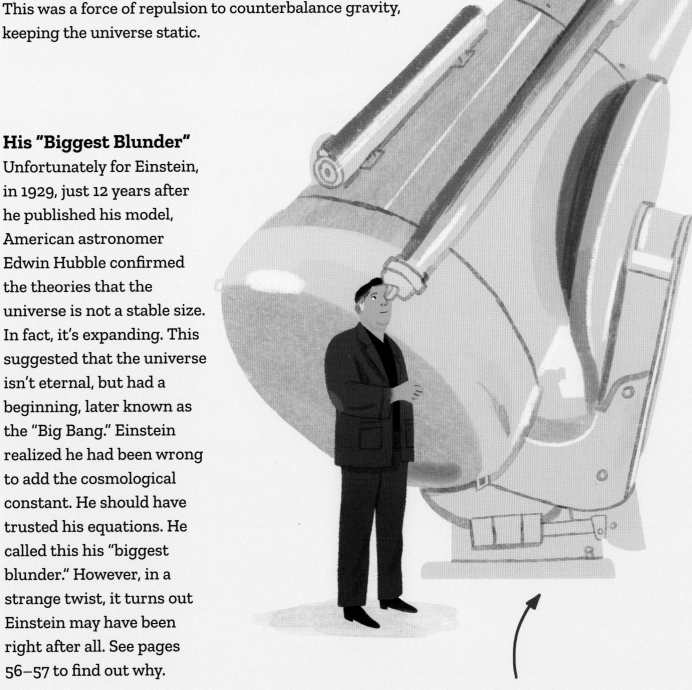

WITH THE GIANT TELESCOPE AT THE MOUNT WILSON OBSERVATORY IN CALIFORNIA, EDWIN HUBBLE FOUND THAT THE GALAXIES ARE RUSHING AWAY FROM EACH OTHER.

QUANTUM THEORY

In the 1890s, physicists were wrestling with the problem of how hot objects emit energy. Energy is emitted in waves, which are measured in wavelengths—the distance between the crest of one wave and the next. The wavelengths of energy emitted by hot objects did not agree with their theories. Shorter wavelengths ought to mean more energy emitted; but in fact, objects emitted less energy at short wavelengths. In 1900, a German physicist called Max Planck came up with a solution.

MAX PLANCK

Planck's Discovery

Planck split the total energy being emitted by the hot object into separate packets. Using this approach, he created a formula that agreed with his observations of how hot objects emit energy. He showed that energy can only be emitted or absorbed in discrete (separate) quantities, or "quanta."

Quantum mechanics is certainly imposing. But an inner voice tells me that it is not yet the real thing.

Albert Einstein, in a letter to Max Born (December 4, 1926).

Light Quanta

Planck's idea inspired Einstein to suggest in the first of his famous 1905 papers that light is also made up of quanta (later called "photons"). The energy of each photon is determined by its wavelength. Einstein did this to solve the problem of the photoelectric effect (see pages 46–47). Until then, physicists had viewed light as a wave. Einstein was saying that it can also behave like a particle. With this insight, he helped launch a whole new branch of physics: quantum mechanics.

Matter Waves

In 1923, Indian physicist Satyendra Bose showed a way of counting photons using Planck's formula. Einstein extended this counting method to atoms, and immediately saw that matter could also behave like a wave.

LOOKING: ELECTRON IS A PARTICLE

The Uncertainty Principle

Around this time, physicists were discovering interesting new properties of atoms. They developed equations that described the actions of atoms and subatomic particles called "electrons," and they found that electrons sometimes behaved like waves and sometimes behaved like particles. Even stranger, they found that an electron's location cannot be known with certainty at the same time as its speed and direction. This is known as the uncertainty principle. Curiously, an electron only occupies a location in space while it is being observed. This is when it behaves like a particle. The rest of the time its position is uncertain—like a wave.

NOT LOOKING: ELECTRON IS A WAVE

Playing Dice

Einstein was troubled by the uncertainties of quantum physics. "God doesn't play dice with the universe," he said. With new discoveries, he was sure it would all make sense. But Einstein was wrong. At the quantum level, the universe is a very strange and uncertain place.

THE PHOTOELECTRIC EFFECT

Einstein's first paper of his miracle year of 1905 offered a solution to a problem in physics known as the "photoelectric effect." The effect had first been observed by the German physicist Heinrich Hertz in 1887. Hertz observed that an electrically charged piece of metal loses its charge more quickly when you shine a light on it.

Light on Metal

This relationship between light and electricity was explained in 1902 by another German physicist, Philipp Lenard. He showed that if you shine light with a short wavelength on a piece of electrically charged metal, it ejects electrons from the metal's surface. It will do so however bright or faint the light is. Increase the brightness of the light, and more electrons are ejected, but it doesn't affect the electrons' energy. If the light is of too long a wavelength, no electrons will be ejected, however bright the light.

Two Problems

According to the accepted theory at the time, light was a wave, and making a light brighter increases the energy it emits. This ought to increase the energy with which each individual electron is emitted. Yet this was not what scientists were observing. There were two problems. First, why does the photoelectric effect only work below a certain wavelength? Second, why does a light's brightness not affect the electrons' energy?

HEINRICH HERTZ

Light as a Particle

Einstein solved both problems by proposing that light, as well as behaving like a wave, could also behave like a particle (later called a "photon"). When you shine a light at a piece of metal, you are bombarding it with photons. Some of these photons will strike electrons on the metal's surface, and the photons' energy will eject the electrons.

A Photon's Energy

Einstein explained that the energy of a photon is related to its wavelength—the longer the wavelength, the lower its energy. This solves the first problem, because if the light has too long a wavelength, the photons will lack sufficient energy to eject electrons. It also solves the second problem, because if a photon's energy is related to its wavelength, then increasing the light's brightness won't increase the photon's energy; it will simply bombard the metal with more photons of the same energy. This will knock more electrons free, but won't make them any more energetic.

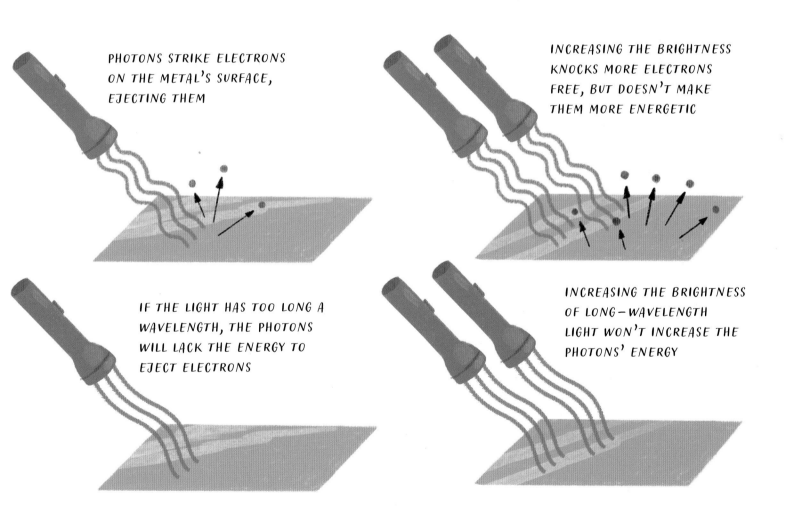

PHOTONS STRIKE ELECTRONS ON THE METAL'S SURFACE, EJECTING THEM

INCREASING THE BRIGHTNESS KNOCKS MORE ELECTRONS FREE, BUT DOESN'T MAKE THEM MORE ENERGETIC

IF THE LIGHT HAS TOO LONG A WAVELENGTH, THE PHOTONS WILL LACK THE ENERGY TO EJECT ELECTRONS

INCREASING THE BRIGHTNESS OF LONG—WAVELENGTH LIGHT WON'T INCREASE THE PHOTONS' ENERGY

Einstein's paper on the photoelectric effect would win him the Nobel Prize for Physics in 1922.

ATOMS AND MOLECULES

The second of the groundbreaking papers that Einstein published during his miracle year of 1905 helped prove the existence of atoms and molecules (groups of atoms bonded together). He did this by explaining the motion of tiny particles in water, known as "Brownian motion."

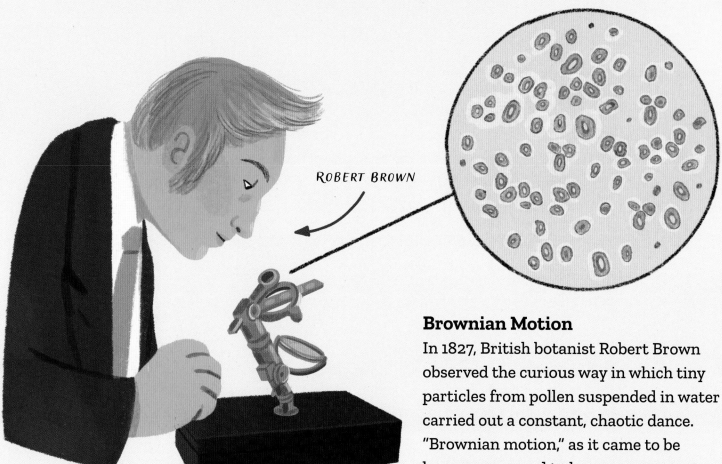

ROBERT BROWN

Brownian Motion

In 1827, British botanist Robert Brown observed the curious way in which tiny particles from pollen suspended in water carried out a constant, chaotic dance. "Brownian motion," as it came to be known, appeared to have no cause, yet it continued endlessly, never slowing down. This puzzled scientists, because it seemed to violate the laws of physics. What invisible energy was driving these particles?

Statistical Approach

Some scientists believed that Brownian motion might demonstrate the existence of atoms and molecules. They thought the particles might be moving because they were being jostled by invisible water molecules. Austrian physicist Ludwig Boltzmann developed a form of statistics that he used to predict the molecules' movement. However, many scientists at the time did not think statistics could be used to understand the nature of matter. They wanted physical evidence that atoms were causing Brownian motion, and not all scientists accepted that atoms and molecules existed at all.

The Motion of Molecules

Einstein had no doubt about the existence of atoms and molecules, and set out to prove it. Molecules are too small to be seen, but he believed their movements could be derived from the motions of larger particles. On average, the impacts would come from every side equally. But at any single instant, more water molecules would be hitting on one side of the particle than the other, causing its seemingly random motion. Einstein turned this insight into an equation that described the movement of molecules mathematically, and also calculated their size.

Experimental Proof

Einstein believed his theory could be tested in an experiment to see if it agreed with reality. In 1908, French physicist Jean Perrin carried out careful microscope studies of Brownian motion. His experiments confirmed Einstein's theory and proved that matter is made up of atoms.

YOU CAN SEE BROWNIAN MOTION YOURSELF BY WATCHING THE MOVEMENT OF DUST SPECKS IN A SHAFT OF LIGHT. THE SPECKS ARE JOSTLED BY THE MOVING MOLECULES OF THE AIR.

WHAT EINSTEIN HELPED CREATE

Albert Einstein's theories of relativity have greatly advanced our understanding of the universe, but his work has also had a practical impact on our lives. Several of the technologies we use today resulted from Einstein's ideas.

Lasers

Lasers are used every day to scan prices in supermarkets, cut through steel, or perform delicate eye surgery. They came from an idea Einstein had in 1917 when he was trying to understand how light interacted with matter. An atom in an excited, or high-energy, state can emit a photon. Einstein wondered if photons liked to move in step, so if a lot of photons were moving in one direction, maybe a high-energy atom would emit a photon in the same direction. Experiments proved him right. A laser works using this process. It excites atoms with light or electrical energy, then channels the photons they emit in a single direction.

Solar Energy

Today, we use solar energy to power spacecraft and generate electricity on Earth. The basis of all solar energy is the photoelectric effect, explained by Einstein in 1905 (see pages 46–47). It was Einstein who showed that packets of light called photons kicked electrons off a surface. In the case of solar energy, the surface is a solar cell. When photons from the Sun strike the cell, they knock electrons free. The electrons move through a material called a semiconductor, producing an electric current.

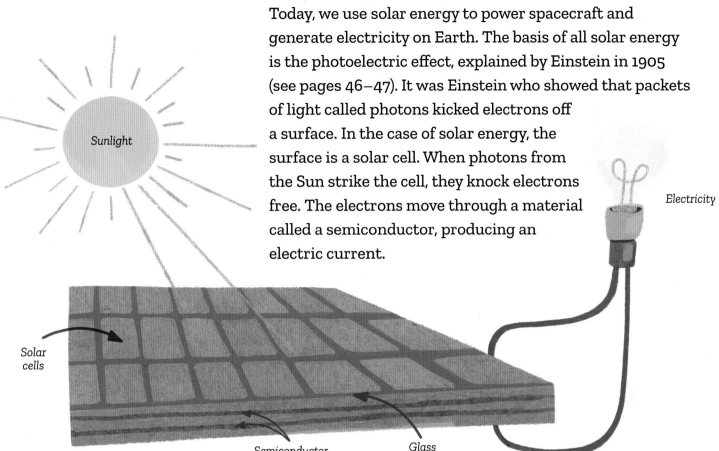

Sunlight

Electricity

Solar cells

Semiconductor

Glass

Accurate GPS

We rely on GPS (Global Positioning System) every day to track our location and movement, to find our way to places, and tell the time. The GPS system is made up of 31 satellites. They emit signals, which are then picked up by a receiver on Earth and used to calculate the receiver's distance from the satellite and determine its position on Earth. The system depends on highly accurate clocks. According to Einstein's general theory of relativity, time is slowed by gravity. So clocks on Earth's surface will run slower than clocks in space. The difference is tiny but measurable. Each day, 38 millionths of a second is added to the satellite clocks to keep them synchronized with those on Earth.

Satellite

Ground station

GPS receiver

THE STATE OF SCIENCE TODAY
BLACK HOLES

KARL SCHWARZSCHILD

Imagine a star bigger than our Sun being squeezed down to a very dense, tiny point. The gravity generated by such a collapsed star would be so powerful that everything, even light, would move towards it. This is a black hole. They were unconfirmed in Einstein's day, yet his general theory of relativity predicted their existence.

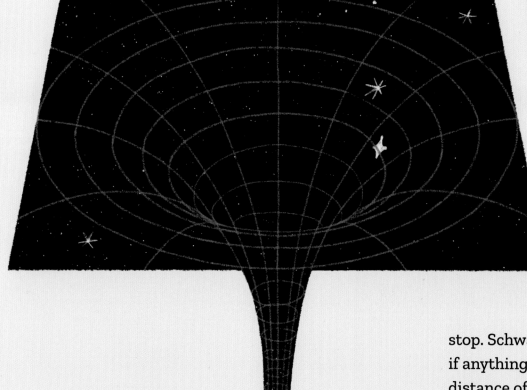

Event horizon

Black hole

Schwarzschild's Discovery

In 1915, German astronomer Karl Schwarzschild provided a solution to Einstein's equations of general relativity, and it showed something very strange. If a star was compressed to a tiny point, spacetime would curve in on itself. At its middle, time itself would stop. Schwarzschild calculated that if anything gets to within a certain distance of such an object, it becomes trapped by it and escape is impossible. The boundary became known as the "event horizon."

Collapsing Stars

Few people at this time believed that such terrifying objects existed—they were just theoretical possibilities thrown up by Einstein's equations. As the twentieth century progressed, astronomers learned how, at the end of a star's life, when it runs out of fuel, its gravity can cause it to collapse. It was likely, therefore, that these objects, later called "black holes," did exist. However, because they gave off no light, they couldn't be seen.

CYGNUS X-1 AND A NEARBY STAR ORBIT EACH OTHER.

Cygnus X-1

In 1964, astronomers discovered a powerful source of X-rays in the sky, but no visible star to explain it. Something that small—the region was much smaller than a star—with so much energy was the first evidence of a black hole. It was named Cygnus X-1.

Different Sizes

Today, astronomers have discovered that the universe contains millions of black holes. Some are the size of an atom, but have the mass of a large mountain. Others, called "stellar black holes," have a mass of up to 20 times that of our Sun. The largest are supermassive black holes, which have masses greater than a million suns. Scientists have found proof that every large galaxy, including our own, has a supermassive black hole at its middle.

WORMHOLES

Take a sheet of paper and write "A" near the top and "B" near the bottom. Now fold the piece of paper in half and punch a hole through it to connect A and B. If the piece of paper represents the universe, you have just created a wormhole—a shortcut between two points in spacetime.

Do Wormholes Exist?

We don't know if they are real—none have ever been found—but Einstein's general theory of relativity predicts they may be possible. The first person to realize this was Austrian physicist Ludwig Flamm in 1916. In 1935, Einstein himself and American–Israeli physicist Nathan Rosen elaborated on Flamm's idea, proposing the possibility of "bridges" through spacetime. They became known as "Einstein-Rosen bridges" or, more popularly, "wormholes."

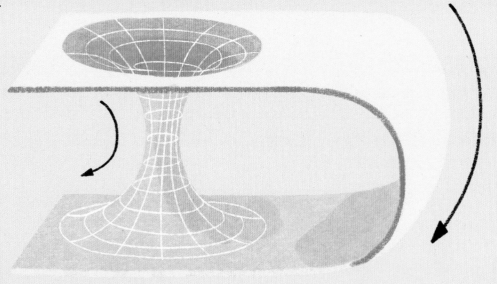

A wormhole could be a way of linking two distant points in spacetime.

What Are They?

Some scientists have speculated that the mouths of a wormhole could be two black holes connecting different parts of the universe, or even two different universes. Between them would be a throat that may be very long or extremely short. Others have suggested that microscopic wormholes could have formed in the early universe. As the universe expands, these could become stretched to larger sizes.

Could We Go Through One?

Wormholes have become a popular feature of science fiction stories, allowing space travel to distant parts of the universe, and even time travel, since they link distant points in both space and time. But could we actually go through one? If wormholes do exist, they would be extremely unstable and likely to collapse very quickly, making them difficult or impossible for a human to pass through.

Exotic Matter

Is it possible to make a wormhole stable? There may exist some form of "exotic matter"—a material not yet discovered—that could keep a wormhole stable for long enough for someone to pass through it. The exotic matter would have to contain enough negative energy to counterbalance the forces trying to collapse the wormhole. So far, scientists have only observed negative energy at microscopic, quantum scales.

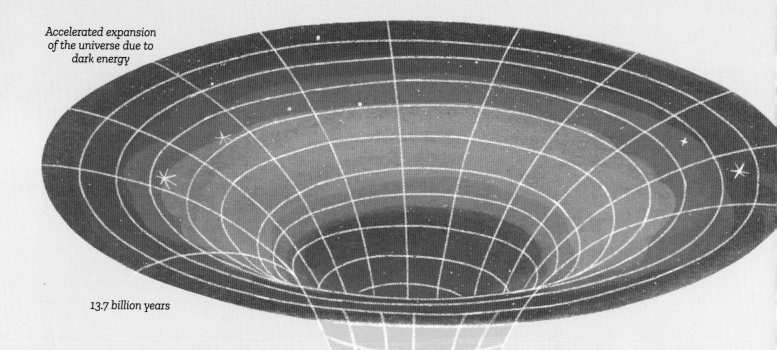

Accelerated expansion of the universe due to dark energy

13.7 billion years

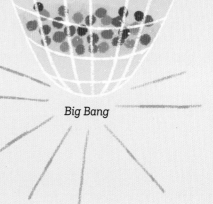

Big Bang

DARK ENERGY

In his equations for general relativity, Einstein added in a repulsive force named the "cosmological constant" (see page 43) to keep the universe static (not expanding or shrinking). He later removed it from his equations, but the latest evidence suggests it might exist after all.

Mysterious Force

In 1998, astronomers discovered that the expansion of the universe is speeding up. This puzzled scientists because, if anything, the expansion ought to be slowing down due to the gravitational pull of all the matter in the universe. It seems that some mysterious force of repulsion is pulling the galaxies apart. We call this force "dark energy." Could it be Einstein's cosmological constant?

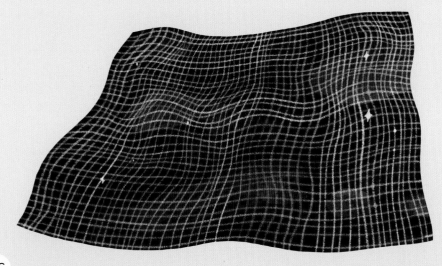

How Much is There?

It has been calculated that roughly 68 percent of the universe is dark energy. Another 27 percent is the equally mysterious "dark matter" (see page 61). Everything we know and observe makes up just 5 percent of the universe.

Is it Virtual Particles?

Space is far from empty. At the extremely small scale, it is full of virtual particles continually popping in and out of existence. Could these give space this dark energy? As the universe expands, more space comes into existence, adding more of this potential energy source, which could cause the expansion to accelerate.

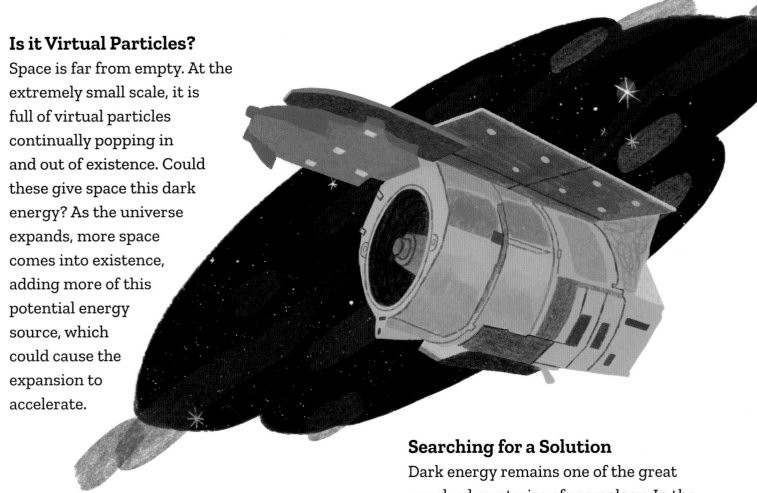

Searching for a Solution

Dark energy remains one of the great unsolved mysteries of cosmology. In the coming years, space missions and ground-based surveys will continue to investigate it and try to work out what it is.

Is it Quintessence?

Some scientists have sugested that dark energy could be an invisible force that fills all of space, yet doesn't interact with anything and cannot be detected. They called this "quintessence."

LEFT TO RIGHT: ADAM RIESS, SAUL PERLMUTTER, AND BRIAN SCHMIDT WON THE NOBEL PRIZE FOR THEIR DISCOVERY OF THE ACCELERATED EXPANSION OF THE UNIVERSE.

RIPPLES FROM SPACE

In 1916, Einstein pointed out another consequence of his general theory of relativity—gravitational waves. His equations showed that massive cosmic events, such as colliding and exploding stars, would send out ripples through the fabric of spacetime. Like stones dropped in a pond, these ripples would go out in all directions, and with the right technology they might be detectable on Earth.

What Causes Them?

Gravitational waves can be caused by a supernova (an exploding star), the orbiting and merging of two black holes, or the orbiting or collision of two neutron stars (small, very dense stars). The waves flow outward from such a phenomenon at the speed of light, carrying information about their origins with them.

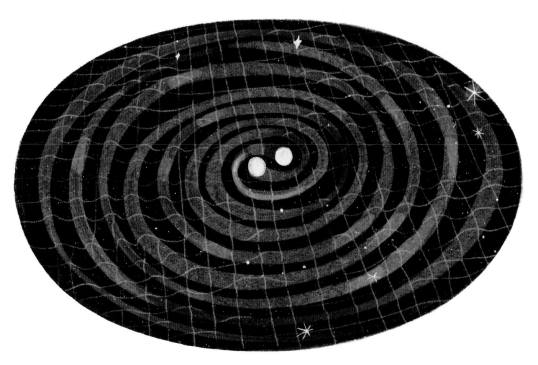

Evidence

The first evidence that Einstein was right about gravitational waves came in 1974, 20 years after his death. Astronomers discovered a binary pulsar (two rotating neutron stars in orbit around each other), exactly the kind of system that could cause gravitational waves. After eight years of observation, they calculated that the stars are moving closer to each other at precisely the rate they ought to be if they are emitting gravitational waves.

The Challenge

We can obtain indirect evidence of gravitational waves through the changing orbits of distant objects. Direct detection is much harder. The waves may result from massive, violent events, but by the time they wash up on Earth, they are extremely weak. In fact, these ripples in spacetime can be a thousand times smaller than the nucleus of an atom! It is therefore quite a challenge to sense their presence.

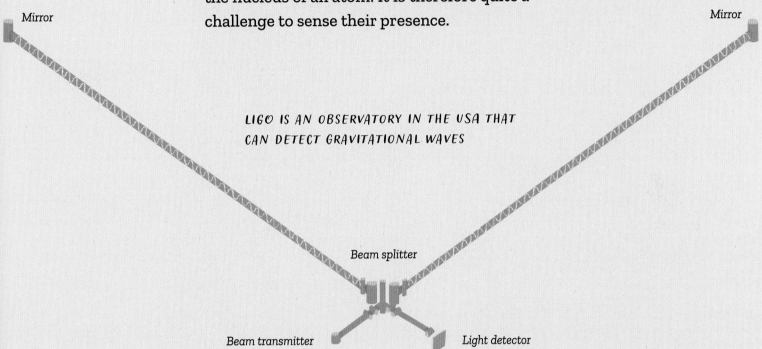

Mirror

Mirror

LIGO IS AN OBSERVATORY IN THE USA THAT CAN DETECT GRAVITATIONAL WAVES

Beam splitter

Beam transmitter

Light detector

Success

The first direct detection of gravitational waves took place in September 2015. This was achieved by a highly sensitive instrument called LIGO (Laser Interferometer Gravitational-Wave Observatory). LIGO has two "arms," each 4 km (2.5 miles) long, with mirrors at either end. The passing waves cause tiny changes in the lengths of the arms detected by laser beams bouncing between the mirrors. The gravitational waves came from two colliding black holes 1.3 billion light years away (a light year is the distance light travels in a year).

What Can We Learn?

Our ability to detect gravitational waves is hugely significant. They can teach us new things about the cosmos and maybe about gravity itself. As Argentinian physicist Gabriela González says, they allow us to "hear the universe."

A THEORY OF EVERYTHING

Einstein spent much of his later career in search of a theory that would capture the workings of the entire universe in a single equation. He ultimately failed in his quest for a "theory of everything," and the challenge was taken up by new generations of physicists.

Relativity Versus Quantum Mechanics

Einstein's general theory of relativity describes the way the universe works at large scales, from the orbit of a planet to the fall of an apple. Here, gravity is the dominant force. Quantum mechanics describes the world on the tiny scale of atoms and subatomic particles, which is governed by three additional forces—electromagnetism, the strong nuclear

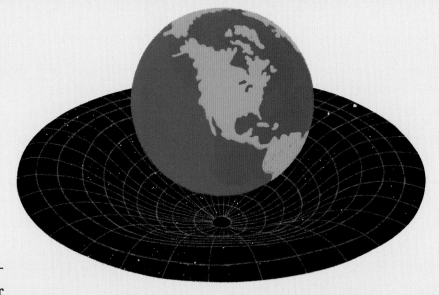

force, and the weak nuclear force. These forces bind molecules, atoms, and their constituent parts together. It seems odd to physicists that the world of the big should work by a different set of rules to the world of the small, and there have been many attempts to marry the two.

String Theory

A promising attempt, starting in the 1980s, was string theory. This proposes that at the beginning of the universe the four fundamental forces were one single force. According to string theory, every particle in the universe, at its most microscopic level, is a vibrating string. The way it vibrates determines whether it's an electron, a photon, or something else. There may well be a gravity particle, but this so-called "graviton" has yet to be found. There have been many versions of string theory, including supersymmetry, supergravity, and M-theory, all with the same aim of uniting gravity with quantum mechanics.

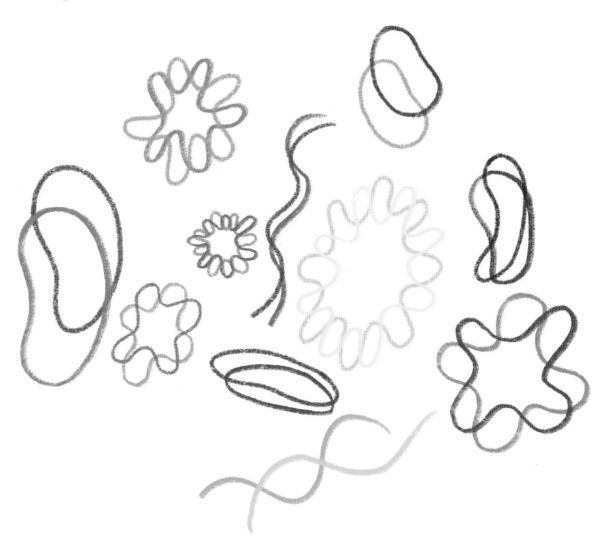

Chasing the Dream

Despite these advances, a convincing theory of everything remains elusive. If it is to be found, it may come from the study of "dark matter," the mysterious, invisible substance that makes up over 80 percent of all matter in the universe. We know it exists, because without it the movements of stars, planets, and galaxies don't make sense. Perhaps if we can find any dark matter particles, it could help us finally unite the laws of physics. Today, scientists following in Einstein's footsteps continue to chase that dream.

GLOSSARY

ABSOLUTE Existing independently and not in relation to other things.

ACCELERATION An increase in speed or rate.

ATOM The smallest part of a chemical element.

ATOMIC BOMB A bomb that gets its destructive power from the rapid release of nuclear energy by the fission (splitting) of atomic nuclei.

COSMOLOGY The science of the origin and development of the universe.

COSMOS The universe.

CURVATURE The way something is curved.

DISCRETE Individually separate.

ELECTROMAGNETISM The interaction of electricity and magnetism, which gives rise to radiation including light, radio waves, and X-rays.

ELECTRON A subatomic particle with a negative charge. It is found in all atoms.

EQUATION A statement that the values of two mathematical expressions are equal, shown by the sign "=" (for example, $E = mc^2$).

EQUIVALENCE The condition of being equal in value or function.

FUSING Joining or blending.

GALAXY A system of millions or billions of stars, held together by gravity.

GEOMETRY The branch of mathematics concerned with the properties and relations of points, lines, surfaces, and solids.

GRAVITY The warping of spacetime that causes bodies with mass to be pulled toward each other.

LENGTH CONTRACTION The shortening of the length of a moving object in the direction of its motion, noticeable when it is close to the speed of light.

MASSIVE BODY A body (such as the Sun) with mass.

MEDIUM The substance through which forms of energy are transmitted.

MOLECULE A group of atoms bonded together.

NUCLEAR Relating to the nucleus of an atom, or to the energy released in nuclear fission or fusion.

NUCLEUS (plural: NUCLEI) The central core of an atom, consisting of protons and neutrons.

ORBIT The curved path of an object around a star, planet, or moon.

PARADOX A seemingly absurd or contradictory statement or idea.

PHOTON A particle, or quantum, of light. A photon carries energy related to its wavelength, but has zero mass.

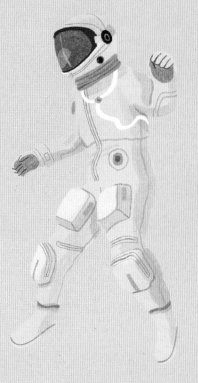

PHYSICS The branch of science concerned with the nature and properties of matter and energy.

QUANTUM (plural: QUANTA) Energy, such as light, in the form of discrete packets.

RELATIVITY The dependence of things like space, time, and gravity on the relative motion of the observer.

REPULSION A force that causes objects to move away from each other.

SOLAR ECLIPSE Blocking of the Sun's light by the Moon moving in front of it.

SPACETIME Time and the three dimensions of space considered as one four-dimensional thing.

STATIC Unchanging.

STATIONARY Not moving.

SUBATOMIC PARTICLE A particle smaller than or occurring within an atom.

SYNCHRONIZED Adjusted to show exactly the same time as another clock or clocks.

THOUGHT EXPERIMENT A hypothetical (not necessarily real or possible) situation laid out in order to think through its consequences.

TIME DILATION The slowing of time as perceived by one observer compared to another, due to the differences in their relative motion.

TURBINE A wheel or rotor made to revolve by a fast-moving flow of water, steam, air, or other fluid in order to generate power.

UNIFORM MOTION Motion in a straight line at a steady speed.

WARP Bend, curve, or twist.

WAVELENGTH The distance between successive crests of an electromagnetic wave, such as a light or radio wave.

X-RAY An electromagnetic wave of high energy and very short wavelength.

INDEX